MATHWORKS!

Using Math to Create a MOVIE STUNT

GARETH STEVENS
PUBLISHING
A World Almanac Education Group Company

by
Wendy and David Clemson
and Joss Gower

Please visit our web site at: www.garethstevens.com
For a free color catalog describing Gareth Stevens Publishing's list of high-quality books and multimedia programs, call 1-800-542-2595 (USA) or 1-800-387-3178 (Canada). Gareth Stevens Publishing's fax: (414) 332-3567.

Library of Congress Cataloging-in-Publication Data

Clemson, Wendy.
    Using math to create a movie stunt/ by Wendy Clemson, David Clemson, and Joss Gower. — North American ed.
        p. cm. — (Mathworks!)
    ISBN 0-8368-4211-1 (lib. bdg.)
    1. Mathematics—Problems, exercises, etc.—Juvenile literature. 2. Stunt performers—Juvenile literature.
    I. Clemson, David. II. Gower, Joss. III. Title. IV. Series.
    QA43.C659   2004
    510'.76—dc22   2004048123

This North American edition first published in 2005 by
Gareth Stevens Publishing
A World Almanac Education Group Company
330 West Olive Street, Suite 100
Milwaukee, Wisconsin 53212

This U.S. edition copyright © 2005 by Gareth Stevens Inc. Original edition copyright © 2004 by ticktock Entertainment Ltd. First published in Great Britain in 2004 by ticktock Media Ltd., Unit 2, Orchard Business Centre, North Farm Road, Tunbridge Wells, Kent, TN2 3XF, England.

The publishers thank the following consultants for their kind assistance: Steve Truglia (stuntman and stunt coordinator), Jenni Back and Liz Pumfrey (NRICH Project, Cambridge University), and Debra Voege (Science and Math Curriculum Resource Teacher).

Gareth Stevens Editor: Dorothy L. Gibbs
Gareth Stevens Art Direction: Tammy West
Illustrator: Stewart Johnson

Photo credits (t=top, b=bottom, c=center, l=left, r=right)
Alamy: cover, 2-3, 7(tr, br), 21(cr), 22-23(c), 23(b), 26-27(c). Bickers Action: 15(bl), 25(tr). Corbis: 15(c). Joe Jennings (Skydive.tv): 1, 16-17. Stewart Johnson: 19. Peter Hassall: 8-9, 21(c). Steve Truglia (prostunts.net): 6-7(c), 10-11, 13, 20.

Every effort has been made to trace the copyright holders for the photos used in this book. The publisher apologizes, in advance, for any unintentional omissions and would be pleased to insert the appropriate acknowledgements in any subsequent edition of this publication.

Printed in the United States of America

1 2 3 4 5 6 7 8 9 08 07 06 05 04

CONTENTS

HAVE FUN WITH MATH

How to Use This Book

Math is important in the daily lives of people everywhere. We use math when we play games, ride bicycles, or go shopping, and everyone uses math at work. Imagine you are a stunt performer and have been asked by a movie director to leap from a building. You may not realize it, but a stuntman or stuntwoman would use math to make sure the stunt looked dangerous but was done safely. In this book, you will be able to try lots of exciting math activities as you learn how movie stunts are made. If you can work with numbers, measurements, shapes, charts, and diagrams, then you could CREATE A MOVIE STUNT.

What does being in the movies feel like?

Grab your safety gear and find out what it is like to crash a car or jump out of a plane!

Math Activities

The stunt coordinator's clipboards have math activities for you to try. Get your pencil, ruler, and notebook (for figuring out problems and listing answers).

MONEY MATTERS

Today, the "car bail out" is being filmed. A hidden stunt driver is driving the car along the pier at 10 to 20 mph. The car has been specially modified so there is room in the front seat for the driver and the two stunt doubles. At exactly the right moment, the stuntman and stuntwoman dive out of the car and land on crash mats that have been placed along the car's route. When the film is edited, shots of the bail out will be blended with close-ups of the lead actors' faces and film of the car hitting the boat. With clever editing, it will look as if the two stars of the movie jumped from the car, themselves, as the car crashed through the end of the pier.

Stunt File

An important part of a stunt coordinator's job is making sure that a stunt can be performed on budget. After a long day working on the set, you still have paperwork to do!

In the DATA BOX on page 23, you will see the costs for the "Countdown" movie stunt. Use this information to make the following budget calculations:

1) What is the cost of the stuntman and stuntwoman if they work on the set for two days?
2) How much will the divers cost if it takes them four days to recover the wreckage?
3) How much more does the speedboat cost than the test boat?
4) How much more does a stunt double earn than the stunt driver if they both work two days?
5) If all the work takes two days, how much will the total stunt budget be? (Remember to include the vehicles, the stunt performers, and the crew.)

Tricks of the Trade

Cars used in stunts can be rigged so that it is possible to drive them from the passenger side or even from behind the driver's seat. Sometimes, the real driver's seat is taken out and replaced with a smaller seat. A hidden stunt performer, covered with a fabric that matches the car's upholstery, then sits on the small seat and drives the car. The stunt driver is actually camouflaged as a car seat!

Stunt Facts

The car door and the area around the door are carefully checked for anything that might catch on the stunt performers' clothing as they dive away from the car. The stuntman and stuntwoman wear protective padding under their costumes. Some stunt performers will even wear thin helmets hidden under a wig.

NEED HELP?

- If you are not sure how to do some of the math problems, turn to pages 28 and 29, where you will find lots of tips to help get you started.

- Turn to pages 30 and 31 to check your answers.
(Try all the activities and challenges before you look at the answers.)

- Turn to page 32 for definitions of some words and terms used in this book.

DATA BOX Stunt Budget

stunt driver (to drive the car and truck)	$900 per day
stunt double for actor	$1,300 per day
stunt double for actress	$1,300 per day
two divers (to recover car and boat wreckage)	$700 each, per day
wardrobe person	$175 per day
five safety officers	$175 each, per day
truck for towing car and boat (rental cost)	$450 per day
speedboat for film shoot	$18,000
Ferrari "kit car" for film shoot	$27,000
test boat for practicing the stunt	$3,500
test car for practicing the stunt	$3,500

Math Challenge

Before preparing a detailed plan, a stunt coordinator must be able to make estimates of what will happen in a stunt.

Use your estimating skills to choose which measurement in each of the following questions is closest to what might actually happen.

1) A speeding stunt car travels at
a) 50 mph b) 500 mph c) 5 mph

2) When a driver presses on the brake pedal, the car begins to stop after
a) 4 seconds b) ¼ second
c) 40 seconds

3) The length of a stuntman's arm is
a) 6 inches b) 20 inches
c) 34 inches

In the movie, the lead actor will drive a real Ferrari, which costs hundreds of thousands of dollars. For the stunt work, a much cheaper "kit car" (replica) will be used.

23

Math Facts and Data

To complete some of the math activities, you will need information from a DATA BOX, which looks like this.

Math Challenge

Purple boxes, like this one, have extra math questions to challenge you. Give them a try!

You will find lots of amazing details about movie stunt performances in FACT boxes that look like this.

IN THE MOVIES

Doing movie stunts is like being paid to play — dangerously! Movie stuntmen and stuntwomen get to smash up expensive vehicles and do seemingly impossible feats, such as climbing tall buildings, driving cars off cliffs, and leaping from airplanes. Stunt performers also get to play a wide variety of characters, including police officers, aliens, astronauts, and gladiators! They appear on movie screens, acting alongside the world's biggest stars, and their names are listed in the credits of major film and television productions. Many stunt performers receive fan mail, just like the famous actors and actresses for whom they double. Sometimes, they are even asked to sign autographs.

Stunt File

Stunt performers travel to locations all over the world. They are involved in designing movie sets, they help special effects artists set up explosions, and they advise actors and directors on how to safely carry out dangerous stunts and film dramatic action shots.

Use the information in the DATA BOX on page 7 to answer the following questions about a stunt performer's day.

1) Where is the stuntman at these times of day?
   a) 10:55 a.m. b) 7:50 a.m. c) 7:47 p.m.
2) How long is the stuntman on the set after lunch?
3) What is the total amount of time allowed for coffee breaks throughout the day?
4) How long was the stuntman "in wardrobe?"

Stuntman Steve Truglia practices a gladiator sword fight.

Tricks of the Trade

To keep fit, stunt performers participate in sports that are good for all-around fitness, such as running and swimming, as well as sports that involve lots of stretching, such as gymnastics, martial arts, and yoga. Being strong and fit helps stuntmen and stuntwomen develop the confidence they need to perform difficult stunt moves.

A Day on the Set

The clocks in this timetable show the starting time for each activity during a stuntman's day filming a movie.

two-mile run

shower and breakfast

arrive on the set

in wardrobe

on the set: practicing sword fight

coffee break

on the set: practicing sword fight

lunch

on the set: filming sword fight

coffee break

on the set: filming sword fight

filming stops for the day

SCUBA training

dinner

Many stunt performers learn martial arts, such as judo and kickboxing.

Circus skills, such as trapeze and high-wire walking, can be useful for some stunts.

Stunt Work Fact

Good stunt performers have a wide range of physical and gymnastic skills. They also learn special skills, such as trampolining, skydiving, rock climbing, falling down stairs (without hurting themselves), sword fighting, and bareback horse riding.

Math Challenge

Every week, a stuntwoman spends 14 hours training for all the special skills she uses in her job. Complete the following statements:

1) Every 2 weeks, she spends ? hours training.
2) Every 3 weeks, she spends ? hours training.
3) Every 10 weeks, she spends ? hours training.

HIGH FALLS

A woman falls from the roof of a building. She screams, waves her arms, and somersaults as she plummets toward the ground, 80 feet below. This fall is not some terrible accident — the woman is a stunt performer, filming a dramatic "high fall" for a movie. Every second of the fall has been carefully planned, tested, and rehearsed. As the director shouts "cut," the stuntwoman makes a perfect landing in the middle of a huge air bag. Besides learning how to fall, stuntmen and stuntwomen have to learn how to land. If a stunt performer does not land in the right position, he or she could be badly injured. If he or she misses the landing rig, the fall could be fatal.

Stunt File

Whenever a stunt is rehearsed or filmed, a safety spotter, who is normally another stunt person, keeps watch from outside the shot. If a stunt performer gets into trouble, the spotter must be ready to rush in and help.

A team of stuntmen and stuntwomen are going to practice high falls. In the DATA BOX on page 9, you will see the places from which they will be jumping. You are one of the safety spotters. Your first job is to help check the positions of all of the landing rigs around the set.

1) In which square should an air bag be placed if a stuntman is jumping from the edge of the parapet?

2) In which square should crash mats be placed if a stuntwoman is jumping to the bottom of the fire escape?

3) In which squares should landing rigs be placed if:
   a) a stuntwoman is falling from anywhere on the balcony?
   b) a stuntman is jumping from the window ledge?

A high fall ends on a gigantic air bag.

Stunt Fact

Most actors do not perform their own stunts because, if they get injured, they may not be able to complete the movie or television show. Trained stuntmen and stuntwomen "double" the actors and perform in any scenes that are dangerous or require special skills.

Stunt Work Fact

Landing rigs can be air bags, thick foam crash mats, or huge stacks of cardboard boxes. An air bag has side vents that release some of the air as the stunt performer lands, which helps the person sink into the bag rather than bounce, possibly off the bag.

8

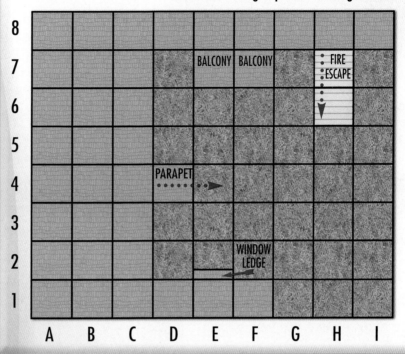

DATA BOX

High Fall Safety Checks

This grid is an aerial view of the set that the stunt team is using to practice their high falls.

	A	B	C	D	E	F	G	H	I
8									
7				BALCONY	BALCONY			FIRE ESCAPE	
6									
5									
4				PARAPET					
3									
2					WINDOW LEDGE				
1									

Math Challenge

Stunt performers use different size air bags for falls from different heights.

1) When planning a high fall, there must be enough room on the set for the right size air bag. What is the area of each air bag?

	AIR BAG DIMENSIONS		
height of fall	length	width	height
30 feet	12 feet	8 feet	4 feet
50 feet	14 feet	12 feet	6 feet
70 feet	15 feet	14 feet	8 feet
100 feet	25 feet	20 feet	10 feet
150 feet	30 feet	25 feet	15 feet

2) You can figure out how much air is in a bag by multiplying the length of the bag times the width, times the height. The answer will be in cubic feet. How many cubic feet of air is in the air bag used for a fall of 100 feet?

After a high fall, the airbag is deflated and carefully rolled up by the stunt crew.

FIRE BURNS

When you watch a movie villain burst into flames, it's easy to forget that a real person is under all that fire and smoke. Fire burns are performed only by experienced stuntmen and stuntwomen, with a large safety team of fire fighters, paramedics, and stunt crew members with fire extinguishers standing by. There are two types of fire burns — partial burns and full-body burns. When performing full-body fire burns, stunt performers are completely covered with special fireproof clothing. They must also hold their breath so they will not accidentally breath in the flames, which could seriously injure or even kill them!

Stunt File

Timing is crucial when performing fire burns. Today, you are assisting in a fire burn stunt as the timekeeper.

The stuntman will be on fire for 20 seconds and has to perform the following actions:

- open a door
- fall forward
- roll over
- get up, then fall again

Then the safety crew will put out the fire.

You must check that everything the stuntman has to do can be completed within 20 seconds.

1) If it takes 8.5 seconds to open the door, how much time is left for the stunt?

2) It takes the stuntman 3.2 seconds to fall forward and 4.8 seconds to roll over. How much time is left now?

3) Your watch shows 11:07 and 55 seconds at the beginning of the stunt. What is the time when the fire burn is over?

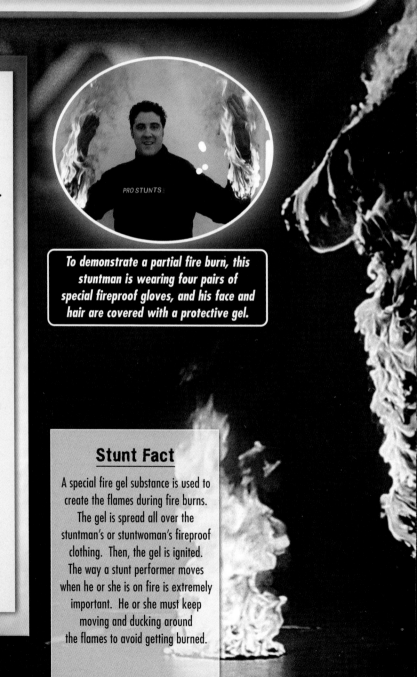

To demonstrate a partial fire burn, this stuntman is wearing four pairs of special fireproof gloves, and his face and hair are covered with a protective gel.

Stunt Fact

A special fire gel substance is used to create the flames during fire burns. The gel is spread all over the stuntman's or stuntwoman's fireproof clothing. Then, the gel is ignited. The way a stunt performer moves when he or she is on fire is extremely important. He or she must keep moving and ducking around the flames to avoid getting burned.

Tricks of the Trade

When doing full-body fire burns, stuntmen and stuntwomen wear special suits made from fire-resistant materials, such as Nomex or Kevlar. They also wear masks that are made from a special silicon mixture. Heat-resistant glass is used in the mask's eyeholes to protect the stunt performer's eyes. During fire burns, a special antiseptic gel is spread over any exposed areas of skin. The gel is cooled in a refrigerator for a few hours before the stunt, so it helps keep the stunt performer's skin cool as the fire heats up. If stunt performers do get burned, the antiseptic is working on their skin right away. Sometimes, for full burns, stunt performers will soak their heat-resistant underwear in the gel and leave it in the refrigerator overnight.

Stuntman Steve Truglia performs a full-body fire burn. The heat of this burn was estimated at 1,472° Fahrenheit.

Math Challenge

Fire burn stunts for films normally last about 20 seconds. During this time, stunt performers must act out their roles, move around the right way to avoid burns, and remember to hold their breath. They are under a lot of pressure and must concentrate hard.

See how well you can concentrate under pressure. Which of the following tasks can you do in 20 seconds? (Ask a friend to time you, or time yourself.)

1) Starting at zero, count by 5s to 500.
2) Say the six times multiplication table backwards, starting with "ten times six."
3) Write the word STUNTMAN and mark which letters show line symmetry.

STUNT DRIVING

An action movie would be a big disappointment if it did not include at least one car chase or one dramatic crash! Stunt drivers learn how to maneuver vehicles at high speeds, without risking any injury to themselves, other actors, or crew members. They also learn how to position or stop a vehicle on an exact spot, called a mark. Movie and television plots require stunt drivers to propel vehicles off buildings, drive on just two wheels, crash into other vehicles, and miss people and objects with just inches to spare. Stunt drivers must also be able to perform exciting high-speed moves, such as skids, spins, and handbrake turns.

Stunt File

If a stunt driver misses the mark, he or she could crash into a camera, a piece of the set, or even a person!

A stuntwoman is asked to make four maneuvers in her car.
She must slide the car and stop on a mark at an exact angle.

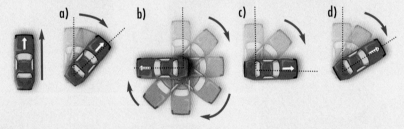

1) To what angle has the car turned each time?

Next, the stuntwoman must reverse at high speed. At the right moment, she uses the handbrake and the steering wheel to make the car skid. As she slides around, she puts the car into first gear and speeds away without having stopped or slowed down.

2) How many degrees has the car turned?

3) Look at this maneuver. How many degrees has the car turned here?

DATA BOX
Stopping Distances

SPEED	STOPPING DISTANCE (number of car lengths)
20 miles per hour (mph)	3
30 mph	6
40 mph	9
50 mph	13
60 mph	18
70 mph	24

A stunt driver and a stuntman work together to perform a "car hit."

Math Challenge

A stunt driver is asked to make a high-speed stop directly in front of a stuntwoman. The driver will plan and test the stunt as follows:

- First, drive along at the required speed, then slam on the brakes.
- Measure how long it takes to slide to a stop and use this "stopping distance" measurement to figure out where the stuntwoman will stand and how far away from the stuntwoman to apply the brakes.
- Practice the stop several times to make sure the stopping distance is the same each time.
- Test the stunt thoroughly, then go for the shot!

Use the information in the DATA BOX above to answer these questions about measuring stopping distances.

1) If the stuntman's car is 10 feet long and is being driven at 50 mph, what is the stopping distance in feet?
2) A stunt car traveling at 30 mph takes 90 feet to stop. How long is the car?
3) A car is 13 feet long. At what speed is it traveling if the driver takes 315 feet to stop?

Tricks of the Trade

For stopping on a mark, especially in front of a person, a wire rope will often be attached to both the rear of the car and a fixed object, such as a tree or a truck. The wire rope is an added safety measure to ensure that the car does not accidentally overrun its mark and hit something — or someone!

STUNT COORDINATORS

Stunt coordinators are the experts who design and arrange stunts. They are generally former stuntmen or stuntwomen who have lots of experience. Because they work with special effects artists, set designers, and even costume and makeup people, stunt coordinators must understand what all the different units working on a film project do. Stunt coordinators must also find the right stunt performers for each job. Then, they have to rehearse with the stunt performers and make sure that the stunt stays on budget. When preparing or filming a stunt, the stunt coordinator is responsible for the safety of all performers and crew on the set.

Stunt File

The map to the right shows five routes that a stunt coordinator is considering for a car chase.

The stunt coordinator has been timing the routes and has written some calculations on the map. Follow each of the routes. As you pass through a calculation, figure out the missing number and write it down in your notebook. Add the calculation totals for each route to find out how many seconds each car chase will last.

Stunt Facts

Anyone watching a movie should not know that a stunt double has taken the place of an actor. In a high fall stunt, the actor is filmed standing at the top of the building, but the stuntman makes the fall. The stunt coordinator has to make sure that the positions and movements of both performers are exactly the same so, in the finished film, no one can tell that two different people played the same character in that scene.

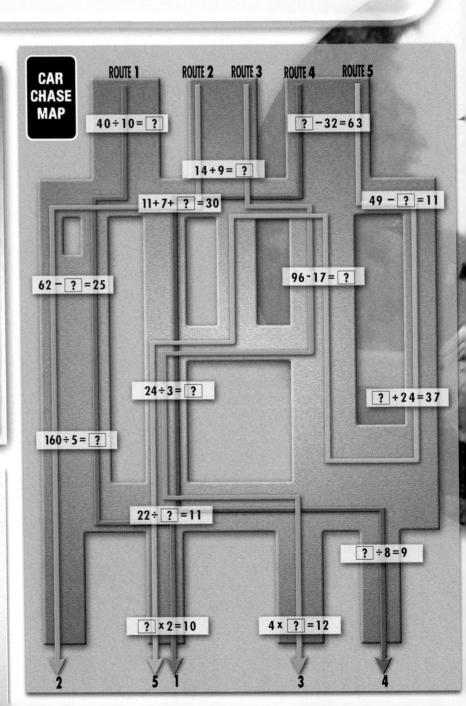

CAR CHASE MAP

ROUTE 1   ROUTE 2   ROUTE 3   ROUTE 4   ROUTE 5

$40 \div 10 = \boxed{?}$

$\boxed{?} - 32 = 63$

$14 + 9 = \boxed{?}$

$11 + 7 + \boxed{?} = 30$

$49 - \boxed{?} = 11$

$62 - \boxed{?} = 25$

$96 - 17 = \boxed{?}$

$24 \div 3 = \boxed{?}$

$\boxed{?} + 24 = 37$

$160 \div 5 = \boxed{?}$

$22 \div \boxed{?} = 11$

$\boxed{?} \div 8 = 9$

$\boxed{?} \times 2 = 10$

$4 \times \boxed{?} = 12$

2   5 1   3   4

Motorcycle Stunt Riders

Stunt motorcycle riders make incredibly long, highly dangerous jumps.
They use takeoff and landing ramps, or they land in huge piles of cardboard boxes!

STUNTMAN	STUNT	LENGTH OF JUMP
Jason Rennie	Made a record-breaking ramp-to-ramp jump on July 9, 2000.	253 feet
Doug Danger	Jumped an L-1011 jumbo jet, wing tip to wing tip, on March 18, 2000.	1,920 inches
Johnny Airtime	Jumped a moving train, head on. (The train went under him.)	180 feet
Robbie Knievel	Jumped a gorge (about 1,500 feet deep) at the Grand Canyon.	2,736 inches
Doug Danger	Jumped 42 cars in 1991.	3,012 inches
Johnny Airtime	Jumped off a ramp to land on a truck that was moving at 60 mph.	135 feet

Stuntman, Greg Brazzell, drives a car into a delivery truck!

A high-speed tracking vehicle is used in filming car chases to carry camera operators and their equipment.

Math Challenge

Many top motorcycle stunt riders attempt long-distance jumps to set records and to WOW audiences at special live shows.

Use the DATA BOX above to find the information you need to answer the following questions:

1) Which jump was the longest?
2) How long was Doug Danger's jumbo jet jump in feet?
3) How long was the shortest jump in meters?

AERIAL STUNTS

Sometimes a movie plot or an idea for a television commercial requires action that takes place thousands of feet above the ground. Stunt coordinators who specialize in skydiving plan and carry out dramatic, and sometimes bizarre, aerial stunts. Stunt skydivers jump from airplanes, helicopters, or high cliffs, accompanied by specially trained camera operators, who film the action using helmet-mounted cameras. The stunt performers act out their roles according to the script, while camera operators capture their maneuvers on film — all while free-falling toward Earth at about 120 mph!

Stunt File

Today, you are part of a team that has to film an aerial stunt for a pizza delivery commercial. When you jump from the plane, you and your camera operator will have just over a minute of free fall time to get the required shots before you need to open your parachutes.

As you exit the plane, you are 16,000 feet above the ground. You will be free-falling at about 1,000 feet every 5 seconds.

1) How far will you free-fall in one second?
2) How far will you free-fall in ten seconds?
3) At an altitude of 2,500 feet, you open your parachute. How far did you fall in free fall?
4) How many seconds were you free-falling before you opened your parachute?

Stunt Heroes

One of the most dangerous and expensive aerial stunts ever filmed was created for the Sylvester Stallone movie "Cliffhanger." Stuntman Simon Crane moved from one jet plane to another at an altitude of 15,500 feet. The stunt cost one million dollars to film.

Aerial cinematographer Joe Jennings films a free fall.

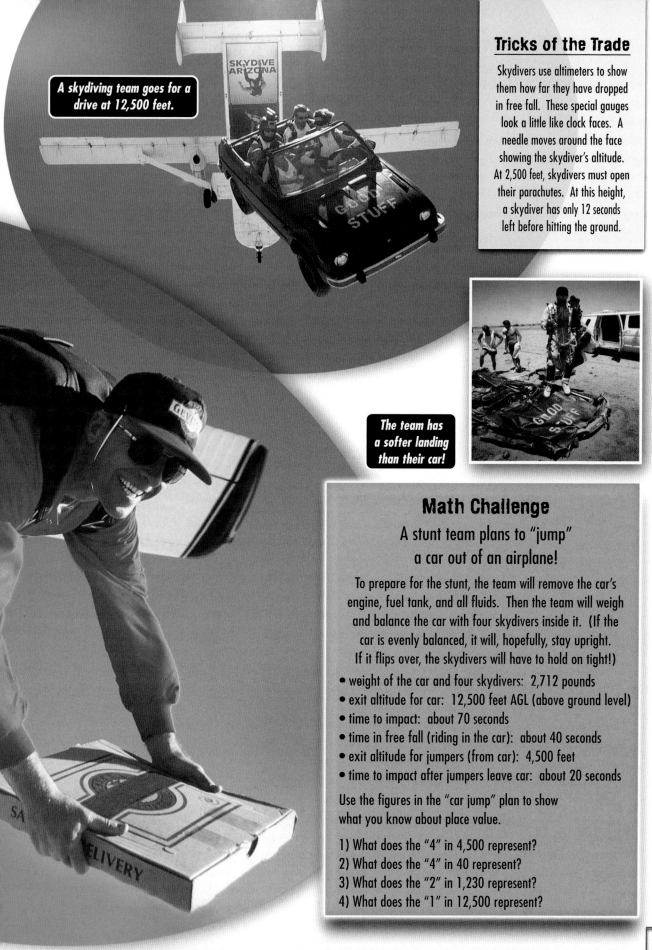

A skydiving team goes for a drive at 12,500 feet.

Tricks of the Trade

Skydivers use altimeters to show them how far they have dropped in free fall. These special gauges look a little like clock faces. A needle moves around the face showing the skydiver's altitude. At 2,500 feet, skydivers must open their parachutes. At this height, a skydiver has only 12 seconds left before hitting the ground.

The team has a softer landing than their car!

Math Challenge

A stunt team plans to "jump" a car out of an airplane!

To prepare for the stunt, the team will remove the car's engine, fuel tank, and all fluids. Then the team will weigh and balance the car with four skydivers inside it. (If the car is evenly balanced, it will, hopefully, stay upright. If it flips over, the skydivers will have to hold on tight!)

- weight of the car and four skydivers: 2,712 pounds
- exit altitude for car: 12,500 feet AGL (above ground level)
- time to impact: about 70 seconds
- time in free fall (riding in the car): about 40 seconds
- exit altitude for jumpers (from car): 4,500 feet
- time to impact after jumpers leave car: about 20 seconds

Use the figures in the "car jump" plan to show what you know about place value.

1) What does the "4" in 4,500 represent?
2) What does the "4" in 40 represent?
3) What does the "2" in 1,230 represent?
4) What does the "1" in 12,500 represent?

A NEW PROJECT

A top director wants you to arrange a nail-biting final sequence for a new action movie. A villain is speeding toward a crowded beach in a speedboat packed with explosives. The movie's two heroes will stop the speedboat by driving their car off the end of a pier and crashing it into the boat. The stunt will make a truly explosive end to the movie. All you have to do is figure out how to make it happen! Getting a car to hit a stationary target is easy, but the boat will be moving at high speed. Also, there will be two stunt performers in the car and a driver in the boat. How will you keep them from being injured?

Stunt File

You have a brilliant plan for this stunt!

A truck will tow both the car and the boat, using a clever system of pulleys and wires attached to the vehicles. When the truck moves forward, the car and the boat will move together, at the same speed, on a collision course. As the car reaches the end of the pier, its wire will be released, but the car will keep moving off the end of the pier and hit the boat. With this plan, there is no need to have anyone in the car or the boat!

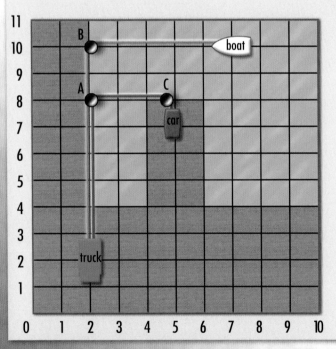

The grid map on the left shows how the car and the boat will be pulled together. Before attempting the stunt, however, you have to figure out some final details.

1) What is the length, in squares, from the truck to pulley A?
2) What is the total length, in squares, of the cable joining the boat and the truck?
3) What are the grid coordinates of
   a) the boat? b) pulley wheel B? c) the truck?
4) What is at point (2,8) on the grid map?
5) What do you think the coordinates will be at the point where the car hits the boat?

Math Challenge
Use the grid map and the compass above to answer the following questions:
1) Which vehicle is southeast of pulley B?   2) Which vehicle is southwest of pulley C?

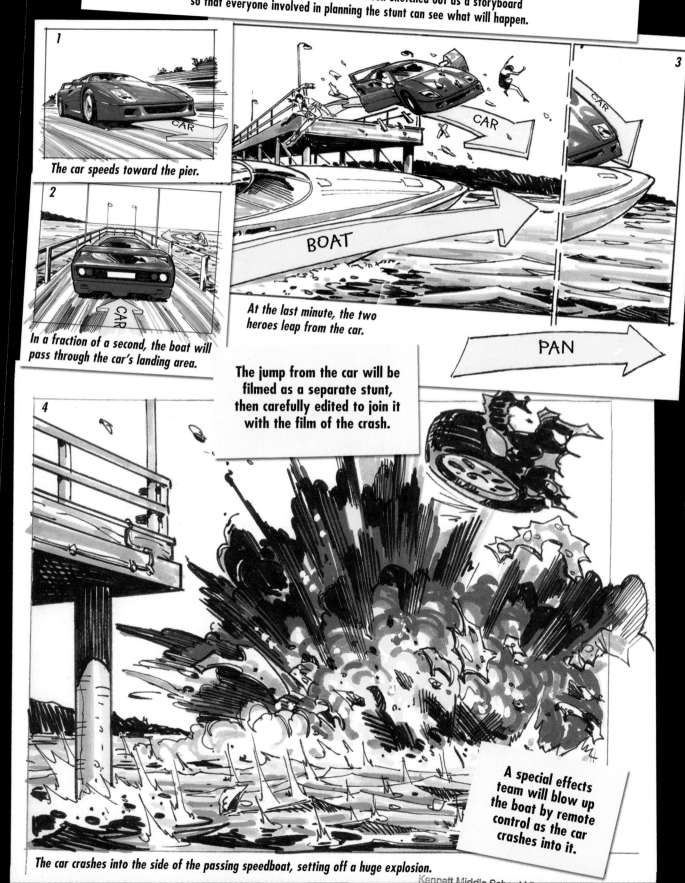

The final sequence of the movie has been sketched out as a storyboard so that everyone involved in planning the stunt can see what will happen.

1 The car speeds toward the pier.

2 In a fraction of a second, the boat will pass through the car's landing area.

At the last minute, the two heroes leap from the car.

3

BOAT

CAR

PAN

The jump from the car will be filmed as a separate stunt, then carefully edited to join it with the film of the crash.

4 The car crashes into the side of the passing speedboat, setting off a huge explosion.

A special effects team will blow up the boat by remote control as the car crashes into it.

FINDING STUNT PERFORMERS

Your idea for the explosive ending is a big success! The director wants you to be the stunt coordinator for his movie, which will be called "Countdown." Shooting will begin soon, so you must start working, immediately, on the details for the stunt. One of your main tasks will be to find a stuntman and a stuntwoman to double the two lead characters. All stunt performers have resumés. This document contains information about their stunt skills, their past work, and their physical characteristics. Movie and television directors, casting agents, and stunt coordinators read performers' resumés to help them choose stunt doubles for particular actors or find stuntmen or stuntwomen with special skills.

hair color — | — height

— eye color

Resumés contain information about a performer's physical appearance.

weight and build

shoe size —

Stunt File

In the DATA BOX on page 21, you will see resumés for five stuntmen.

1) Which stuntman has rock climbing skills and brown hair?

2) Which stuntman has not done street fighting but can skydive and is more than 6 feet tall?

3) Who would you not choose to double for an actor who is more than 6 feet tall?

4) Who would you choose to double in a fire burn stunt for an actor who is 5 feet, 11 inches tall and weighs 225 pounds?

The DATA BOX contains descriptions of stunt skills needed for three projects.

5) Which stuntmen have the right skills for
a) the television commercial?
b) the hospital drama?
c) the movie "Countdown"?

Tricks of the Trade

Sometimes, a stuntman or a stuntwoman will wear a wig, extra padding, or a disguise to look more like the actor he or she is doubling.

DATA BOX Stuntmen Resumés

STUNTMAN	ALEC	PAUL	DAVID	CHRIS	ED
height:	5 feet 10 inches	6 feet 5 inches	5 feet 10 inches	6 feet 2 inches	5 feet 11 inches
weight:	175 pounds	216 pounds	232 pounds	225 pounds	198 pounds
shoe size:	9	11	9	10	9
hair color:	blond	brown	brown	black	brown
eye color:	brown	brown	brown	blue	brown
STUNT SKILLS	fire burns car bail outs street fighting rock climbing skateboarding	car bail outs car hits stair falls skydiving rock climbing	fire burns sword fighting car hits street fighting car bail outs	bareback horse riding saddle falls skydiving cowboy fighting street fighting	bungee jumping skateboarding skydiving car bail outs trapeze

"COUNTDOWN" ACTOR	"COUNTDOWN" STUNTS	HOSPITAL DRAMA STUNTS	TV COMMERCIAL STUNTS
height: 5 feet 10 inches weight: 175 pounds shoe size: 9 hair color: brown eye color: brown	fire burn car bail out street fighting	car hit stair fall rock climbing	skydiving trapeze skateboarding

Stuntmen and stuntwomen must look as much like the actors and actresses they are doubling as possible.

A stuntman and stuntwoman are learning how to fight.

Math Challenge

In the DATA BOX above, you will see a description for the lead actor in the movie "Countdown."

Which of the stuntmen would be the best double for this actor?

MONEY MATTERS

Today, the "car bail out" is being filmed. A hidden stunt driver is driving the car along the pier at 10 to 20 mph. The car has been specially modified so there is room in the front seat for the driver and the two stunt doubles. At exactly the right moment, the stuntman and stuntwoman dive out of the car and land on crash mats that have been placed along the car's route. When the film is edited, shots of the bail out will be blended with close-ups of the lead actors' faces and film of the car hitting the boat. With clever editing, it will look as if the two stars of the movie jumped from the car, themselves, as the car crashed through the end of the pier.

Stunt File

An important part of a stunt coordinator's job is making sure that a stunt can be performed on budget. After a long day working on the set, you still have paperwork to do!

In the DATA BOX on page 23, you will see the costs for the "Countdown" movie stunt. Use this information to make the following budget calculations:

1) What is the cost of the stuntman and stuntwoman if they work on the set for two days?
2) How much will the divers cost if it takes them four days to recover the wreckage?
3) How much more does the speedboat cost than the test boat?
4) How much more does a stunt double earn than the stunt driver if they both work two days?
5) If all the work takes two days, how much will the total stunt budget be? (Remember to include the vehicles, the stunt performers, and the crew.)

Tricks of the Trade

Cars used in stunts can be rigged so that it is possible to drive them from the passenger side or even from behind the driver's seat. Sometimes, the real driver's seat is taken out and replaced with a smaller seat. A hidden stunt performer, covered with a fabric that matches the car's upholstery, then sits on the small seat and drives the car. The stunt driver is actually camouflaged as a car seat!

Stunt Facts

The car door and the area around the door are carefully checked for anything that might catch on the stunt performers' clothing as they dive away from the car. The stuntman and stuntwoman wear protective padding under their costumes. Some stunt performers will even wear thin helmets hidden under a wig.

In the movie, the lead actor will drive a real Ferrari, which costs hundreds of thousands of dollars. For the s[tunt] work, a much cheaper "kit car" (replica) will be use[d].

Math Challenge

Before preparing a detailed plan, a stunt coordinator must be able to make estimates of what will happen in a stunt.

Use your estimating skills to choose which measurement in each of the following questions is closest to what might actually happen.

1) A speeding stunt car travels at
   a) 50 mph b) 500 mph c) 5 mph

2) When a driver presses on the brake pedal, the car begins to stop after
   a) 4 seconds b) ¼ second
   c) 40 seconds

3) The length of a stuntman's arm is
   a) 6 inches b) 20 inches
   c) 34 inches

I t is early morning on the day of the crash shoot. The speedboat is anchored in the harbor, and the car is in position at the dock. Both vehicles are attached, by long wires, to the tow bar of a huge truck. With the stunt rigged (set up), the camera crew is making its final preparations. Cameras are mounted on tripods, as well as on tracks running along the pier. A camera mounted on a huge crane will film a dramatic aerial shot of the crash. Out in the harbor, a cameraman on board a helicopter is ready to film the explosion. Every second of the stunt will be caught on film from every possible angle.

Stunt File

The grip crew are the experts who rig (set up) the cameras for filming a movie or TV show and move the cameras around during filming.

One way to move a camera is to use a dolly, which is a special kind of trolley that looks like a platform on four wheels. Sometimes, a track similar to a train track is used for moving a camera. The camera is mounted on a dolly that moves up and down the track.

1) This section of a track shows small camera movements.
   Estimate the position of the camera for each shot.

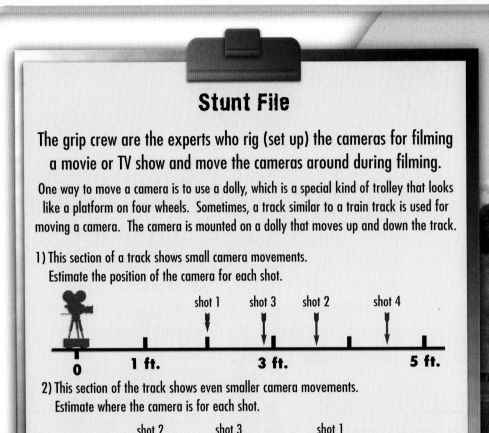

2) This section of the track shows even smaller camera movements.
   Estimate where the camera is for each shot.

Tricks of the Trade

To film actors inside a moving car, a camera can be mounted on the hood of the vehicle to film through the windshield. A camera can also be mounted on a "hostess tray" (named after the trays that, at one time, were commonly used at drive-in restaurants) positioned on the side of the car. The action is filmed through the driver's or passenger's window.

Tricks of the Trade

When filming a moving vehicle, the "picture car," which is the vehicle being filmed, can be mounted on a low trailer and towed. The position of the picture car still looks natural in relation to the road. Towing is a safe way to film moving vehicles because the actors do not have to perform and drive at the same time.

With the taxi on the trailer, camera operators can film the action in the vehicle from inside the trailer's special cab.

Math Challenge

On a film set, crews can spend a lot of time waiting for other crews to do their jobs.

While the cameramen and the grip crew set up the cameras, take a break and try to figure out the questions for the answers on this crossword puzzle.

ACROSS
1. 6 x 8 =
4. 7 x 9 =
6. 8 x 9 =
7. 8 x 8 =

DOWN
1. 7 x 7 =
2. 9 x 9 =
3. 7 x 8 =
5. 9 x 4 =

SHOOTING A TAKE

The cameras are in place, and the special effects crew has set up the explosion. Everyone is ready for a take. The director shouts "action," and the truck starts to move forward, pulling the boat and the car. The vehicles go faster and faster. When the car reaches the end of the pier, its wire is released. The car soars through the air toward the boat. As the two vehicles impact, a special effects pyrotechnician sets off the explosion by remote control. Flames, smoke, and pieces of car and boat fly through the air. The director shouts "cut." The crew claps and cheers. The stunt has worked perfectly. It's a wrap!

Stunt File

The stunt team's work is finished.
Now the divers can begin their work,
recovering the wreckage of the boat and car.

Some pieces of debris recovered from the harbor
after the explosion are pictured below.
Look at the shapes carefully and answer the questions that follow.

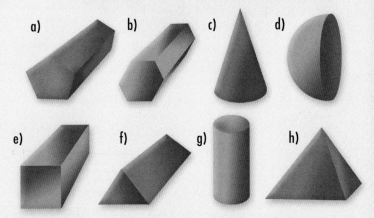

a)   b)   c)   d)

e)   f)   g)   h)

1) The cone (c) has an apex. Which other shape has an apex?
2) Which shapes have at least one circular face?
3) Which shapes are prisms?
4) How many straight edges does each prism have?
5) What can you say about the total number of edges for each prism?

Stunt Fact

The area around a stunt shoot is blocked off by safety officers to keep members of the public from wandering onto the movie set when a stunt is being filmed.

Tricks of the Trade

Filming an explosion usually means having only one chance to get it right! The special effects crew puts an explosive device on board the speedboat. When it is detonated, the explosive charge breaks up the body of the boat. To create a dramatic, highly visual explosion, pyrotechnicians have also put fuel and a special black powder inside the boat.

Math Challenge

For a stunt to be successful, the sequence of events has to be planned carefully.

Try to complete these number sequences to see how good you are at putting things in the right order.

1) What are the next three numbers?
   a) 12, 19, 26, 33, _ , _ , _
   b) 101, 104, 107, 110, _ , _ , _
   c) 32, 29, 26, 23, _ , _ , _

2) What are the missing numbers?
   a) _ , _ , 36, 40, _ , 48, _
   b) 16, 7, _ , −11, _ , _

MATH TIPS

PAGES 8-9

Stunt File

The grid diagram in the DATA BOX on page 9 is not the same as a map grid that is used to find exact points. This grid is used to find, approximately, where things are. On a grid of a town, for example, you could find out where, or in which areas (squares), shops are located.

Math Challenge

Two ways to do multiplication are:
THE GRID METHOD

12 x 8

8 x 10	8 x 2	
80	16	= 96

PARTITIONING

14 x 12

```
              14
         x    12
14 x 10      140
14 x 2        28
             168
```

This diagram illustrates a cubic foot.

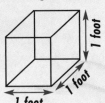

1ft x 1ft x 1ft = 1 cubic foot

TOP TIP: One foot is 12 inches or approximately 30 centimeters.

PAGES 10-11

Stunt File

TOP TIP: There are 60 seconds in one minute.

PAGES 12-13

Stunt File

An "angle" is a measure of turning that is expressed in degrees. The symbol for degrees is °.

One complete turn (a complete revolution) is 360°, and one complete revolution has four right angles (90°).

TOP TIP: Use a protractor to measure angles.

Math Challenge

Using car lengths is a way to find approximate stopping distances. Other factors, such as road conditions and tire quality, also affect stopping distances.

PAGES 14-15

Stunt File

To find missing numbers, it helps to remember that, for every number statement, there are three related number statements. If we know, for example, that

8 x 2 = 16

then we can also write the following statements:

2 x 8 = 16
16 ÷ 2 = 8
16 ÷ 8 = 2

The missing number in any of these statements could be 2, 8 or 16, depending on the position of the missing number and whether the statement is multiplication or division.

PAGES 16-17

Stunt File

TOP TIP: To find the answer to question 4, you need to figure out how many units of 1,000 feet are in the total distance of your freefall. Then, multiply this number by the number of seconds it takes to fall 1,000 feet.

PAGES 18-19

Stunt File

The grid map is a rough diagram of the stunt plan. To use a grid map, read along the bottom first, then read up the side.

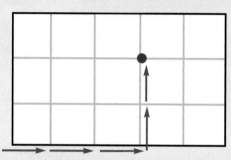

Example: To find a grid reference at point (3,2), move 3 squares along the bottom, then 2 squares up.

PAGES 20-21

Stunt File

When comparing different sets of information, making a chart, like the one below, can be helpful.

STUNTMAN	SKILLS		
	car bail out	fire burn	skydiving
1	✔	✔	
2	✔		✔
3	✔	✔	
4			✔
5	✔		✔

PAGES 22-23

Math Challenge

An estimate is not a guess. It is an answer that we know will be close to what is exactly correct. Being good at estimating can help you figure out math problems and check your answers.

PAGES 24-25

Stunt File

A number line is continuous and extends forever in both directions. The length of the line can be decided according to the numbers with which you are working. Here is a line extending from 0.1 to 0.2 with some points marked in between.

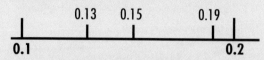

0.13   0.15   0.19

0.1   0.2

PAGES 26-27

Stunt File

A prism is a solid shape with each side exactly the same size and shape all along its length. If you slice through a prism, the cut faces will be the same size and shape as the ends of the prism. A rectangular prism is called a cuboid.

Math Challenge

TOP TIP: When looking at sequences, try to figure out the difference between pairs of numbers to find the pattern.

ANSWERS

PAGES 6–7

Stunt File

1) a) 10:55 a.m.: on the set, practicing a sword fight
   b) 7:50 a.m.: in wardrobe
   c) 7:47 p.m.: at SCUBA training
2) After lunch, the stuntman is on the set for 5 hours and 15 minutes
3) A total of 55 minutes is allowed for coffee breaks.
4) The stuntman was in wardrobe for 30 minutes.

Math Challenge

The stuntwoman spends the following amounts of time in training:
1) every 2 weeks, 28 hours
2) every 3 weeks, 42 hours
c) every 10 weeks, 140 hours

PAGES 8–9

Stunt File

1) E4 2) H6 3a) D7, D6, E6, F6, G6, G7
3b) D2, E2, F2

Math Challenge

1) Area of air bags:
   96 square feet (30-foot fall)
   168 square feet (50-foot fall)
   210 square feet (70-foot fall)
   500 square feet (100-foot fall)
   750 square feet (150-foot fall)
2) This bag has 5,000 cubic feet of air.

PAGES 10–11

Stunt File

1) 11.5 seconds   2) 3.5 seconds
3) 11:08 and 15 seconds

Math Challenge

3) T U T M A

PAGES 12–13

Stunt File

1) a) 45° b) 270° c) 90° d) 60°
2) The car has turned 180°.
3) The car has turned 360°.

Math Challenge

1) The stopping distance is 130 feet.
2) The car is 15 feet long.
3) The car is traveling at 70 mph.

PAGES 14–15

Stunt File

ROUTE 1	ROUTE 2	ROUTE 3
$40 \div 10 = 4$	$14 + 9 = 23$	$14 + 9 = 23$
$62 - 37 = 25$	$11 + 7 + 12 = 30$	$96 - 17 = 79$
$160 \div 5 = 32$	$62 - 37 = 25$	$24 \div 3 = 8$
$22 \div 2 = 11$	$160 \div 5 = 32$	$4 \times 3 = 12$
$5 \times 2 = 10$	sum of totals is 110	sum of totals is 122
sum of totals is 82		

ROUTE 4	ROUTE 5
$95 - 32 = 63$	$95 - 32 = 63$
$11 + 7 + 12 = 30$	$49 - 38 = 11$
$24 \div 3 = 8$	$13 + 24 = 37$
$22 \div 2 = 11$	$96 - 17 = 79$
$72 \div 8 = 9$	$24 \div 3 = 8$
sum of totals is 121	$22 \div 2 = 11$
	$5 \times 2 = 10$
	sum of totals is 219

Math Challenge

1) Jason Rennie's ramp-to-ramp jump.
2) Doug Danger's jumbo jet jump was 160 feet.
3) The shortest jump, which was Johnny Airtime's moving truck jump, was 41 meters (135 feet).

PAGES 16–17

Stunt File

1) 200 feet   2) 2,000 feet
3) 13,500 feet
4) 67.5 seconds (1 minute and $7\frac{1}{2}$ seconds.)

Math Challenge

1) thousands   2) tens
3) hundreds   4) ten-thousands

PAGES 18–19

Stunt File

1) 5 squares   2) 11 squares
3) a) boat (7,10)   b) pulley wheel B (2, 10)
   c) truck (2,2)
4) Pulley wheel A is at point (2,8) on the grid map.
5) The crash will happen at (5,10).

Math Challenge

1) The car is southeast of pulley B.
2) The truck is southwest of pulley C.

PAGES 20–21

Stunt File

1) Paul   2) Paul   3) Alec, David, and Ed   4) David
5) a) the television commercial: Ed
   b) the hospital drama: Paul
   c) the movie "Countdown": Alec and David

Math Challenge

Alec wearing a brown wig would be the best
stunt double for the "Countdown" actor.

PAGES 22–23

Stunt File

1) $5,200 2) $5,600 3) $14,500 4) $800 5) $52,000

Math Challenge

The following estimates are closest to what actually happens.
1) a (50 mph) 2) b ($\frac{1}{4}$ second) 3) b (20 inches)

PAGES 24–25

Stunt File

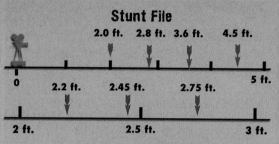

Math Challenge

1. 4	8			8 2.
9		3. 5		1
		4. 6	5. 3	
6. 7	2		7. 6	4

PAGES 26–27

Stunt File

1) pyramid (h)
2) cone (c), hemisphere (d), cylinder (g)
3) pentagonal prism (a), hexagonal prism (b),
   rectangular prism (e), triangular prism (f)
4) triangular prism – 9, rectangular prism – 12,
   pentagonal prism – 15, hexagonal prism – 18
5) It is a a multiple of three, or a product in the
   three times (multiplication) table.

Math Challenge

1) a) 40, 47, 54 b) 113, 116, 119
   c) 20, 17, 14
2) a) 28, 32, 44, 52 b) –2, –20, –29

GLOSSARY

AERIAL from high above or occurring high in the air

ALTIMETERS instruments that measure altitude, which is the vertical height above a surface

APEX a pointed end or tip

CINEMATOGRAPHER a camera operator who specializes in filming motion pictures

COORDINATES sets of numbers that identify specific points or locations on a line or a surface or in a space

DETONATED set off or sparked an explosion

DOUBLE (v) to stand in for, or take the place of, someone else who has similar physical features, especially in situations that are dangerous or that require special skills

EDITED put together separate sections of film in a way that blends them into a continuous sequence of actions

FREE-FALLING moving unrestricted, at great speed, toward the ground during the part of a skydive before opening the parachute

GRIP a film or television technician who rigs, or sets up, the cameras and moves them around during filming

MANEUVER (v) to move or handle skillfully; (n) a carefully controlled movement for a particular purpose

MARK an exact spot on the set of a film or television production that shows a performer precisely where he or she must stand, land, or end up for a particular film shot

PAN to move a motion-picture camera in a way that follows a particular object or action, creating a panoramic effect

PARAPET a low wall or protective barrier, such as along the edge of a roof

PLOT the main story of a book, play, or movie

PLUMMETS drops suddenly and rapidly

PYROTECHNICIAN a special effects expert who works with fire and explosives

RALLY a car race on public roads, using common traffic rules, over a route that is not revealed to participants until the start of the race

RIG (n) equipment that is set up or arranged for a specific use

SCRIPT the text of a production, which includes all lines spoken by the actors as well as basic instructions for the actions

SETS the indoor or outdoor backgrounds or settings for particular scenes in plays, films, or television programs, which can be either real locations or buildings or replicas constructed inside film studios

SHOOTING filming

SHOTS the individual, uninterrupted runs of cameras during filming

STORYBOARD a sequence of drawings or sketches that show the shots planned for one scene of a filmed production

SYMMETRY the property of having balanced and visually similar halves on either side of a line dividing an object

TAKE a scene filmed at one time without stopping the camera

TRIPODS three-legged stands that hold cameras steady while in use

WRAP a completed filming session

Measurement Conversions

1 inch = 25.4 millimeters (mm)

1 inch = 2.54 centimeters (cm)

1 foot = 0.3048 meters (m)

1 cubic foot = 0.0283 cubic meters

1 pound = 0.4536 kilograms

1 mile = 1.609 kilometers

Fahrenheit (F)° − 32° ÷ 1.8 = Celsius (C)°